# Summary

The Patient Protection and Affordable Care Act (ACA) reauthorized new funding for numerous existing discretionary grant and other programs and activities. ACA also created multiple new discretionary grant programs and activities and provided for each an authorization of appropriations. Funding for all of these programs and activities is subject to action by congressional appropriators. This report summarizes all the discretionary spending provisions in ACA that authorized appropriations for grant programs and other activities. A companion product, CRS Report R41301, *Appropriations and Fund Transfers in the Patient Protection and Affordable Care Act (PPACA)*, summarizes all the mandatory appropriations in the new law.

Among the provisions that are intended to strengthen the nation's health care safety net and improve access to care, ACA permanently reauthorized the federal health centers program and the National Health Service Corps (NHSC). The NHSC provides scholarships and student loan repayments to individuals who agree to a period of service as a primary care provider in a federally designated Health Professional Shortage Area. In addition, the new law addressed concerns about the current size, specialty mix, and geographic distribution of the health care workforce. It reauthorized and expanded existing health workforce education and training programs under Titles VII and VIII of the Public Health Service Act (PHSA). Title VII supports the education and training of physicians, dentists, physician assistants, and public health workers through grants, scholarships, and loan repayment. ACA created several new programs to increase training experiences in primary care, in rural areas, and in community-based settings, and provided training opportunities to increase the supply of pediatric subspecialists and geriatricians. It also expanded the nursing workforce development programs authorized under PHSA Title VIII to bolster undergraduate and graduate nursing education and training.

As part of a comprehensive framework for federal community-based (i.e., public health) prevention activities, including a national strategy and a national education and outreach campaign, ACA authorized several new grant programs with a focus on preventable or modifiable risk factors for disease (e.g., sedentary lifestyle, tobacco use). The new law also leveraged a number of mechanisms to improve the quality of health care, including new requirements for quality measure development, collection, analysis, and public reporting; programs to develop and disseminate innovative strategies for improving the quality of health care delivery; and support for care coordination programs such as medical homes, patient navigators, and the co-location of primary health care and mental health services.

Additionally, ACA authorized funding for programs to prevent elder abuse, neglect, and exploitation; grants to expand trauma care services and improve regional coordination of emergency services; and demonstration projects to implement alternatives to current tort litigation for resolving medical malpractice claims, among other provisions.

The Congressional Budget Office estimated that ACA's discretionary spending provisions, if fully funded by future appropriations acts, would result in appropriations of approximately $106 billion over the 10-year period FY2010-FY2019. Most of that funding would be for programs that existed prior to, and whose funding was reauthorized by, ACA. Few new programs created by ACA received funding in FY2011 or FY2012.

# Contents

## Tables

## Contacts

# Introduction

The Patient Protection and Affordable Care Act (ACA)[1] restructured the private health insurance market, set minimum standards for health coverage, created a mandate for most U.S. residents to obtain health insurance coverage, and provided for the establishment by 2014 of state-based health insurance exchanges for the purchase of private health insurance. Qualifying individuals and families will be able to receive federal subsidies to reduce the cost of purchasing coverage through the exchanges. The new law also expanded eligibility for Medicaid; amended the Medicare program in an effort to reduce the rate of its projected growth; imposed an excise tax on insurance plans found to have high premiums; and made many other changes to the tax code, Medicare, Medicaid, the Children's Health Insurance Program (CHIP), and other federal programs.

Implementation of ACA is projected to have a significant impact on federal revenues and direct (also referred to as mandatory) spending.[2] The law included direct spending to subsidize the purchase of health insurance coverage through the exchanges, as well as increased outlays for the expansion of the Medicaid program. ACA also included numerous mandatory appropriations to fund temporary programs to increase access and funding for targeted groups, provide funding to states to plan and establish exchanges, and support many other research and demonstration programs and activities (see discussion below under "Mandatory Appropriations in ACA"). The costs of expanding public and private health insurance coverage and other mandatory spending are offset by revenues from new taxes and industry fees, and by savings from payment and health care delivery system reforms designed to slow the growth in spending on Medicare and other federal health care programs.[3]

ACA implementation will affect not only direct spending and revenue but may also impact discretionary spending, which is subject to the annual appropriations process.[4] The law included numerous discretionary spending provisions that authorize the appropriation of funds to implement grant programs and other activities. These provisions are of two kinds:

- Authorizations of appropriations for *new* discretionary grant and other programs created by ACA.

- Authorizations of appropriations for *existing* programs, primarily ones authorized under the Public Health Service Act (PHSA). In most instances, the appropriation

---

[1] ACA was signed into law on March 23, 2010 (P.L. 111-148, 124 Stat. 119). A week later, on March 30, 2010, the President signed the Health Care and Education Reconciliation Act (HCERA; P.L. 111-152, 124 Stat. 1029), which amended multiple health care and revenue provisions in ACA. Several other bills that were subsequently enacted during the 111th Congress made more targeted changes to specific ACA provisions. All references to ACA in this report refer to the law as amended. Note that previous CRS reports on the Patient Protection and Affordable Care Act used the acronym PPACA to refer to the law. CRS is now using the more common acronym ACA.

[2] Mandatory, or direct, spending generally refers to budget authority (i.e., the authority to incur financial obligations that result in government expenditures, such as purchasing services or awarding grants) that is provided in laws other than the annual appropriations acts. Mandatory spending includes entitlement authority (e.g., Medicare, Social Security).

[3] For more information on ACA's provisions and its projected impact on federal revenues and direct spending, see CRS Report R41664, *ACA: A Brief Overview of the Law, Implementation, and Legal Challenges*, coordinated by C. Stephen Redhead.

[4] Discretionary spending refers to outlays from budget authority that is provided in and controlled by annual appropriations acts.

authorizations for these established programs expired prior to their reauthorization by ACA. However, almost all of them continued to receive an annual appropriation. Note: ACA reauthorized the Indian Health Care Improvement Act (IHCIA), which includes many discretionary Indian Health Service (IHS) programs and services. It also extended indefinitely the authorizations of appropriations for those programs and services. For more information on ACA's Indian health provisions, which are not included in this report, see CRS Report R41630, *The Indian Health Care Improvement Act Reauthorization and Extension as Enacted by the ACA: Detailed Summary and Timeline*, by Elayne J. Heisler.

Many of the ACA discretionary spending provisions authorize annual appropriations of specified amounts for one or more fiscal years to carry out the program or activity. Other provisions authorize the appropriation of specified amounts for FY2010 or FY2011 and unspecified amounts—such sums as may be necessary, or SSAN—for later years. A few provisions authorize multi-year appropriations, available for obligation for a period in excess of one fiscal year (e.g., for the period FY2011 through FY2014). Numerous other provisions simply authorize the appropriation of SSAN, in a few cases without specifying any fiscal years.

Funding for all discretionary programs in ACA depends on actions taken by congressional appropriators, a process that may lead to greater or smaller amounts than the sums authorized by the law. With Congress now operating under discretionary spending limits set by the Budget Control Act, it may prove difficult to secure funding for new programs and activities (see discussion below under "Potential Impact of Automatic Spending Reductions on Discretionary Spending"). Even maintaining current funding levels for existing programs with an established appropriations history may prove a challenge under growing pressure to reduce federal discretionary spending.

This report, which is periodically revised and updated to reflect important legislative and other developments, summarizes all the discretionary spending provisions in ACA that authorize (or reauthorize) appropriations for grant and other programs.

# Discretionary Spending in ACA

The law's discretionary spending provisions are organized by general topic in a series of tables with the following headings: Health Centers and Clinics (**Table 1**); Health Care Workforce (**Table 2**); Prevention and Wellness (**Table 3**); Maternal and Child Health (**Table 4**); Health Care Quality (**Table 5**); Nursing Homes (**Table 6**); Health Data Collection (**Table 7**); Emergency Care (**Table 8**); Elder Justice (**Table 9**); Biomedical Research (**Table 10**); Biologics (**Table 11**); 340B Drug Pricing (**Table 12**); Medical Malpractice (**Table 13**); Pain Care Management (**Table 14**); Medicaid (**Table 15**); Medicare (**Table 16**); and Private Health Insurance (**Table 17**).

Each table row includes the following information: (1) the ACA section number; (2) an indication of whether the provision amends an existing section of the PHSA (or another law), or whether it creates a new program either in the PHSA (or another law) or in new stand-alone statutory authority, as well as the name (if known) of the administering agency or office within the Department of Health and Human Services (HHS); (3) a brief description of the program or activity, including the types of entities and/or individuals eligible for funding;[5] and (4) details of the authorization of appropriations, along with the FY2011 and FY2012 amounts for programs and activities that received funding and, if applicable, the FY2013 funding request.[6] In several of the larger tables with multiple entries, the ACA provisions are grouped based on whether they reauthorize funding for existing program or authorize funding for new programs. Where available, the table entry includes the Catalog of Federal Domestic Assistance (CFDA) number for the grant program.[7] Unless otherwise stated, all references in the tables to the Secretary refer to the HHS Secretary.

The Congressional Budget Office (CBO) estimated that ACA's discretionary spending provisions, if fully funded by future appropriations acts, would result in appropriations of approximately $106 billion over the period FY2010-FY2019.[8] However, much of that funding—about $82 billion—is for three programs that predate ACA and whose funding was reauthorized by the law; namely, the National Health Service Corps, the federal health centers program, and the IHS.

Most, though not all, of the existing grant and other programs that were reauthorized under ACA received a discretionary appropriation for FY2011 and FY2012, as well as a FY2013 request for continued funding. However, it appears that to date only one of the new grant programs authorized under ACA has received annual discretionary appropriations.[9] A handful of other new programs have received mandatory funds from ACA's Prevention and Public Health Fund (see discussion below under "Mandatory Appropriations in ACA").

---

**Acronyms Used in the Tables in This Report**

Agency for Healthcare Research and Quality (AHRQ)

Centers for Disease Control and Prevention (CDC)

Centers for Medicare and Medicaid Services (CMS)

Community Health Center Fund (CHCF)

Federal Food, Drug, and Cosmetic Act (FFDCA)

Food and Drug Administration (FDA)

Health Resources and Services Administration (HRSA)

Indian Health Service (IHS)

National Institutes of Health (NIH)

Office of Personnel Management (OPM)

Office of the Secretary (OS)

Prevention and Public Health Fund (PPHF)

Public Health Service Act (PHSA)

Substance Abuse and Mental Health Services Administration (SAMHSA)

Social Security Act (SSA)

---

[5] Not applicable if the funding is to support programs and activities carried out by a federal agency.

[6] The FY2011, FY2012, and FY2013 (request) funding amounts are taken from HHS agency FY2013 congressional justification documents, available at http://www.hrsa.gov/about/budget/index.html.

[7] CFDA is a government-wide compendium of federal grant and other assistance programs. Each program is assigned a unique five-digit number, XX.XXX, where the first two digits represent the funding agency and the second three digits represent the program. Programs funded by the Department of Health and Human Services begin with the number 93. For more information, see https://www.cfda.gov.

[8] U.S. Congressional Budget Office, letter to the Honorable Jerry Lewis about the potential effects of the Patient Protection and Affordable Care Act on discretionary spending, May 11, 2010, available at http://www.cbo.gov/ftpdocs/114xx/doc11490/LewisLtr_HR3590.pdf. CBO's estimate of discretionary spending includes (1) amounts specified in ACA, plus estimated amounts for subsequent years (adjusted for anticipated inflation) where ACA specifies an amount for the first year (FY2010 or FY2011) and authorizes SSAN for subsequent years; and (2) estimated amounts for subsequent years (adjusted for anticipated inflation) where there is an appropriation under prior law for FY2010 and ACA authorizes the appropriation of SSAN for later years. The CBO estimate does not include new ACA programs for which the law provided only an authorization for the appropriation of SSAN.

[9] That program is the Cures Acceleration Network (CAN) program at the National Institutes of Health, see **Table 10**.

---

In addition to the costs of fully funding ACA's discretionary grant and other programs, CBO projected that both the Department of Health and Human Services (HHS) and the Internal Revenue Service (IRS) will incur substantial administrative costs to implement the law's private health insurance reforms and its changes to the federal health care programs. CBO estimated that the costs to the IRS of implementing the eligibility determination, documentation, and verification processes for the health insurance subsidies will probably total between $5 billion and $10 billion over 10 years. It further estimated that the costs to HHS of implementing the changes in Medicare, Medicaid, and CHIP, as well as some of the reforms to the private insurance market, will require similar amounts over 10 years.[10]

The Health Care and Education Reconciliation Act (HCERA) established and provided $1 billion to the Health Insurance Reform Implementation Fund (HIRIF) to help cover the administrative costs of implementing the law.[11] HHS projects that all the HIRIF funds will have been obligated by the end of FY2012. Thereafter, ACA administrative costs will have to be funded through annual discretionary appropriations.

## Potential Impact of Automatic Spending Reductions on Discretionary Spending

The Budget Control Act of 2011 (BCA) authorized the President to increase the nation's debt limit by at least $2.1 trillion and established procedures designed to reduce future federal spending by a comparable amount.[12] To achieve the spending reductions, the law placed statutory limits, or caps, on discretionary spending for each of FY2012 through FY2021. CBO estimated that adhering to these limits, which grow by approximately 2% each year, would reduce discretionary spending by $917 billion through FY2021, compared to the projected level of spending if annual appropriations were to grow at the rate of inflation.[13]

In addition, the BCA created a Joint Select Committee on Deficit Reduction (Joint Committee) and instructed it to develop deficit-reduction legislation for Congress to consider under expedited floor procedures. If, by January 15, 2012, Congress and the President failed to enact a Joint Committee bill reducing the deficit by at least $1.2 trillion over the period FY2012-FY2021, then automatic annual spending reductions would be triggered beginning in FY2013. The November 21, 2011, announcement by the Joint Committee that it was unable to agree on a deficit-reduction bill means that automatic spending reductions totaling $1.2 trillion are all but certain to take effect, absent any further action by Congress and the President to modify or repeal the BCA.

The automatic spending reductions under the BCA would cut $54.7 billion from both defense and nondefense spending for each fiscal year over the period FY2013-FY2021. The annual spending reduction in each category—defense and nondefense—would be divided proportionately between

---

[10] See footnote 8.

[11] HCERA Section 1105; see footnote 1.

[12] P.L. 112-25, 125 Stat. 240. For a more detailed examination of all the provisions in the BCA, see CRS Report R41965, *The Budget Control Act of 2011*, by Bill Heniff Jr., Elizabeth Rybicki, and Shannon M. Mahan. The President has exercised the authority provided him in the BCA and raised the debt ceiling by a total of $2.1 trillion, from $14.294 trillion to $16.394 trillion.

[13] U.S. Congressional Budget Office, *Analysis of Budget Control Act*, August 1, 2011. Available at http://www.cbo.gov/publication/41626.

discretionary spending and nonexempt direct (i.e., mandatory) spending. In FY2013, both the discretionary and the direct spending reductions would be achieved through sequestration—a largely across-the-board cancellation of budgetary resources in nonexempt accounts. In each of the remaining fiscal years through FY2021, discretionary spending reductions would be achieved through a downward adjustment of the BCA spending limits, while direct spending reductions would continue to be executed through sequestration.

Under the sequestration rules, reductions in Medicare payments to health care providers and health plans (which account for most of Medicare spending) are capped at 2%. Many other federal direct spending programs, accounting for most of the federal government's entitlement and other direct spending (other than Medicare), are exempt from sequestration altogether. The sequestration rules also exempt a few discretionary programs, notably veterans' health care and Pell grants, and cap at 2% any reduction in discretionary spending on health centers and Indian health care.[14]

Nondefense, nonexempt discretionary spending programs, including most of the funded programs summarized in the tables in this report, would be subject to about a 9% reduction under sequestration in FY2013.[15] Again, cuts in spending for health centers would be capped at 2%, and spending on veterans' health care and Pell grants would be exempt altogether. In each year from FY2014 through FY2021, however, the required dollar reduction in discretionary spending would be achieved by lowering the BCA spending caps. There would be no across-the-board cuts through sequestration. Instead, the Appropriations Committees would decide how to apportion the cuts within the reduced cap, and spending on health centers, Indian health, Pell grants and veterans' health care would no longer be protected as they are under the sequestration rules. For more discussion of the spending reductions triggered by the BCA, and the current legislative activity to modify those procedures, see CRS Report R42051, *Budget Control Act: Potential Impact of Automatic Spending Reduction Procedures on Health Reform Spending*, by C. Stephen Redhead.

# Mandatory Appropriations in ACA

Separate from the discretionary spending authorizations discussed in this report, ACA included numerous mandatory appropriations that provide billions of dollars to fund new and existing grant programs and activities within HHS. All these mandatory spending provisions are summarized in a companion product, CRS Report R41301, *Appropriations and Fund Transfers in the Patient Protection and Affordable Care Act (PPACA)*, by C. Stephen Redhead.

Of particular note, ACA established two multi-billion dollar funds that are helping support several of the discretionary grant programs authorized (or reauthorized) under ACA. First, the Community Health Center Fund (CHCF) will provide a total of $11 billion over the period FY2011-FY2015 for the federal health centers program and the National Health Service Corps (NHSC).[16] While CHCF funds have so far been used to supplement annual discretionary

---

[14] For more information, see CRS Report R42050, *Budget "Sequestration" and Selected Program Exemptions and Special Rules*, coordinated by Karen Spar.

[15] Center on Budget and Policy Priorities, "How the Across-the-Board Cuts in the Budget Control Act Will Work," by Richard Kogan. Available at http://www.cbpp.org/files/12-2-11bud2.pdf.

[16] ACA Section 10503(a)-(b). The CHCF provides the following amounts for health center operating grants: FY2011 = (continued...)

appropriations for the health centers program, the NHSC program received no discretionary funding for FY2012 and is relying entirely on CHCF funds (see **Table 1** and **Table 2**). A separate ACA appropriation provided $1.5 billion for health center construction and renovation (see **Table 1**).[17]

Second, the Prevention and Public Health Fund (PPHF), for which ACA provided an annual appropriation in perpetuity, is intended to fund prevention, wellness, and other public health-related programs and activities authorized under the PHSA.[18] PPHF funds have been used to support five new discretionary grant programs authorized under ACA.[19] In addition, PPHF funds are supplementing, and in some cases supplanting, annual discretionary appropriations for several established programs that were reauthorized by the law (see **Table 2**, **Table 3**, and **Table 5**).

---

(...continued)

$1 billion; FY2012 = $1.2 billion; FY2013 = $1.5 billion; FY2014 = $2.2 billion; and FY2015 = $3.6 billion. It also provides the following amounts for the National Health Service Corps: FY2011 = $290 million; FY2012 = $295 million; FY2013 = $300 million; FY2014 = $305 million; and FY2015 = $310 million.

[17] ACA Section 10503(c).

[18] ACA Section 4002. As originally enacted, ACA appropriated the following amounts to the PPHF: FY2010 = $500 million; FY2011 = $750 million; FY2012 = $1 billion; FY2013 = $1.25 billion; FY2014 = $1.5 billion; and FY2015 and each fiscal year thereafter = $2 billion. The Middle Class Tax Relief and Job Creation Act of 2012 (P.L. 112-96, Sec. 3205) amended Section 4002 and reduced the amounts appropriated over the period FY2013-FY2021 by a total of $6.25 billion. The reduced appropriations for each of those fiscal years are as follows: FY2013 = $1 billion; FY2014 = $1 billion; FY2015 = $1 billion; FY2016 = $1 billion; FY2017 = $1 billion; FY2018 = $1.25 billion; FY2019 = $1.25 billion; FY2020 = $1.5 billion; and FY2021 = $1.5 billion.

[19] Those programs are (1) Sec. 5208, Nurse-Managed Health Clinics, see **Table 1**; (2) Sec. 5306, Mental and Behavioral Health Education and Training Grants, see **Table 2**; (3) Sec. 5102, State Health Care Workforce Development Grants, see **Table 2**; (4) Sec. 4201, Community Transformation Grants, see **Table 3**; and (5) Sec. 10408, Small Business Workplace Wellness Grants, see **Table 3**.

---

## Table 1. ACA Discretionary Spending: Health Centers and Clinics

| ACA Section | Statutory Authority (Agency) | Summary of Provision | Authorization of Appropriations; Funding (FY2011-FY2013) |
|---|---|---|---|
| **Health Centers: Existing Program** | | | |
| 5601 | Reauthorizes PHSA Sec. 330 (HRSA) | **Health centers.** Permanently reauthorizes funding for the program that provides operating grants to health centers serving federally designated medically underserved populations and furnishing comprehensive primary care services, referrals, and other services needed to facilitate access to such care, regardless of ability to pay. Eligible grantees include community, migrant, public housing, and homeless health centers that meet the statutory requirements of PHSA Sec. 330. | $3.0 billion for FY2010, $3.9 billion for FY2011, $5.0 billion for FY2012, $6.5 billion for FY2013, $7.3 billion for FY2014, and $8.3 billion for FY2015; amounts in subsequent years based on previous year's funding, subject to adjustment. <br><br> *FY2011 funding = $2.6 billion (includes $1.0 billion from the CHCF), FY2012 funding = $2.8 billion (includes $1.2 billion from the CHCF), FY2013 request = $3.1 billion (includes $1.5 billion from the CHCF).*[a] [CFDA 93.224, 93.527] <br><br> Note: ACA Sec. 10503(c) appropriated $1.5 billion for the period FY2011 through FY2015 for health center construction and renovation; see CRS Report R41301. |
| **Health Centers and Clinics: New Programs** | | | |
| 4101(b) | New PHSA Sec. 399Z-1 (HRSA) | **School-based health centers (SBHCs).** Requires the Secretary to award grants to fund the management and operation of SBHCs that provide comprehensive physical and behavioral health services to children and adolescents, subject to parental consent. SBHCs that meet certain specified criteria and match 20% of the grant amount with non-federal funds (unless waived). Preference may be given to SBHCs serving children and adolescents who have limited access to or difficulty accessing health care. | SSAN for each of FY2010 through FY2014. <br><br> Note: ACA Sec. 4101(a) appropriated a total of $200 million for SBHC construction and renovation; see CRS Report R41301. |
| 5208 | New PHSA Sec. 330A-1 (HRSA) | **Nurse-managed health clinics (NMHCs).** Requires the Secretary to award grants to fund the operation of NMHCs—associated with schools, colleges, federally qualified health centers (FQHCs), or nonprofit health/social services agencies—that provide comprehensive primary health care and wellness services to vulnerable or underserved populations regardless of income or insurance status. At least one advanced practice nurse must hold an executive management position in the NMHC. | $50 million for FY2010, and SSAN for each of FY2011 through FY2014. <br><br> Note: This new program received $15 million in FY2010 funds from the PPHF but has not received any funding since that time. [CFDA 93.515] |

| ACA Section | Statutory Authority (Agency) | Summary of Provision | Authorization of Appropriations; Funding (FY2011-FY2013) |
|---|---|---|---|
| 10504 | New authority (HRSA) | **Access to affordable care demonstration program.** Within six months of enactment, requires the Secretary to establish a three-year demonstration project in up to 10 states—each state may receive up to $2 million—to provide access to comprehensive health care services to the uninsured. Eligible grantees must be state-based, nonprofit, public-private partnerships that provide access to comprehensive health care services to the uninsured at reduced fees. | SSAN (no years specified). |

**Sources:** Table prepared by the Congressional Research Service based on the text of the Patient Protection and Affordable Care Act (ACA; P.L. 111-148, as amended). FY2011, FY2012 and requested FY2013 funding amounts are taken from HRSA's FY2013 congressional justification document, available at http://www.hrsa.gov/about/budget/index.html.

a. Annual funding totals for health centers include the following amounts for the Federal Tort Claims Act (FTCA) program: FY2011 = $100 million; FY2012 = $95 million; FY2013 request = $95 million. Under the FTCA, health center employees and contractors are considered federal employees immune from medical malpractice lawsuits while acting within the scope of their employment. The federal government assumes responsibility for such malpractice claims.

## Table 2. ACA Discretionary Spending: Health Care Workforce

| ACA Section | Statutory Authority (Agency) | Summary of Provision | Authorization of Appropriations; Funding (FY2011-FY2013) |
|---|---|---|---|
| **National Health Service Corps (NHSC)** | | | |
| 5207 | Reauthorizes PHSA Title III, Part D, Subpart III (HRSA) | **NHSC scholarships and loan repayments.** Permanently reauthorizes funding for the NHSC program. In exchange for a commitment to work in a federally designated Health Professional Shortage Area (HPSA), the program provides (1) scholarships to students training in a primary care discipline to cover tuition, fees, other educational costs, and a stipend; and (2) student loan repayments of up to $50,000 a year to primary care and mental health clinicians. To be eligible for a scholarship, a student must be accepted or enrolled in a training program for medicine, dentistry, family nurse practitioner, nurse midwife, or physician assistant, and agree to two to four years of service in an NHSC-approved site in a HPSA. Loan repayments are for primary care, dental, and mental health clinicians who agree to at least two years of service in an NHSC-approved site in a HPSA. | $320 million for FY2010, $414 million for FY2011, $535 million for FY2012, $691 million for FY2013, $893 million for FY2014, and $1,155 billion for FY2015; amounts in subsequent years based on previous year's funding, subject to adjustment.<br><br>*FY2011 funding = $315 million (includes $290 million from the CHCF), FY2012 funding = $295 million (all CHCF), FY2013 request = $300 million (all CHCF).* [CFDA 93.162, 93.288, 93.547] |

| ACA Section | Statutory Authority (Agency) | Summary of Provision | Authorization of Appropriations; Funding (FY2011-FY2013) |
|---|---|---|---|
| **Physicians: Existing Program** | | | |
| 5301 | Amends and reauthorizes PHSA Sec. 747 (HRSA) | **Primary care training and enhancement program.** (1) Authorizes five-year grants to public and nonprofit private hospitals, medical schools, academically affiliated physician assistant training programs, and other public and nonprofit private entities to support training programs in primary care. Funds are to be used to plan, develop and operate accredited training programs, including residency and internship programs, in family medicine, general internal medicine, and general pediatrics and to provide financial assistance (e.g., traineeships). (2) Authorizes five-year grants to medical schools for primary care capacity building. Funds are to be used to create academic units or programs that improve clinical teaching in the primary care fields, and (in a separate authorization) to integrate academic units to enhance interdisciplinary recruitment, training, and faculty development. Funding priority given to entities proposing innovative approaches to primary care training and with a record of training primary care providers, among other things. | For both grant programs, $125 million for FY2010, and SSAN for each of FY2011 through FY2014. Note: 15% of the amount appropriated must be use for physician assistant training programs.<br><br>A separate authorization of $750,000 for each of FY2010 through FY2014 is provided for capacity building grants to integrate academic units.<br><br>*FY2011 funding = $39 million, FY2012 funding = $39 million, FY2013 request = $51 million.* [CFDA 93.510, 93.514, 93.884]<br><br>Note: For FY2010, this program received $198 million in PPHF funds in addition to its annual discretionary appropriation of $39 million. |
| **Physicians: New Programs** | | | |
| 5203 | New PHSA Sec. 775 (HRSA) | **Pediatric specialist loan repayment program.** Requires the Secretary to implement a loan repayment program that pays up to $35,000 for each year of service (for a maximum of three years) to practicing or in-training pediatric specialists and surgeons, as well as child and adolescent mental health specialists, who agree to at least two years of service in a HPSA. | $30 million for each of FY2010 through FY2014 for loan repayments to pediatric specialists and surgeons; $20 million for each of FY2010 through FY2013 for loan repayments to mental health providers.<br><br>*FY2013 request = $5 million.* |
| 5508(a) | New PHSA Sec. 749A (HRSA) | **Teaching health centers development grants.** Authorizes three-year grants of up to $500,000 to FQHCs, rural health clinics, Indian health centers, and entities receiving PHSA Title X (family planning) funds that establish or expand a primary care residency training program. | $25 million for FY2010, $50 million for each of FY2011 and FY2012, and SSAN for each fiscal year thereafter. |
| 10501(l) | New PHSA Sec. 749B (HRSA) | **Rural physician training grants.** Requires the Secretary to (1) award grants medical schools for recruiting students most likely to practice in underserved rural communities and for providing rural-focused training and experience; and (2) within 60 days of enactment, by regulation, define underserved rural communities. Priority is given to entities that train students to practice in rural communities, that have established partnerships with rural community health centers, or who submit a long-term plan for tracking where graduates practice. [Note: HRSA published an interim final rule on May 26, 2010 (75 *Federal Register* 29447).] | $4 million for each of FY2010 through FY2013. |

| ACA Section | Statutory Authority (Agency) | Summary of Provision | Authorization of Appropriations; Funding (FY2011-FY2013) |
|---|---|---|---|
| **Dentistry: Existing Program** | | | |
| 5303 | New PHSA Sec. 748; authority previously part of Sec. 747 (HRSA) | **General, pediatric, and public health dentistry training.** Authorizes grants or contracts to dental and dental hygiene schools, as well as approved residency or advanced education programs in general, pediatric, or public health dentistry, for dental training activities including faculty development, financial assistance, faculty loan repayment programs, technical assistance for pediatric dental programs, and pre- and post-doctoral training programs in dental primary care. Gives priority to entities that train individuals from disadvantaged backgrounds, who have a record of placing graduates in facilities that provide care to the underserved, or whose programs focus on providing care to the underserved through demonstrated partnerships with FQHCs, rural health clinics, or through having programs focused on specific topics, such as HIV/AIDs. | $30 million for FY2010, and SSAN for each of FY2011 through FY2015; permits grantees to carry over funds for up to three fiscal years. *FY2011 funding = $17 million, FY2012 funding = $20 million, FY2013 request = $20 million.* [CFDA 93.059, 93.884] Note: HRSA also administers a state oral health workforce grant program (PHSA Sec. 340G): FY2011 funding = $16 million, FY2012 funding = $12 million, FY2013 request = $11 million. [CFDA 93.236] |
| **Dentistry: New Program** | | | |
| 5304 | New PHSA Sec. 340G-1 (HRSA) | **Alternative dental health care provider demonstration program.** Authorizes the Secretary to award 15 five-year grants of not less than $4 million to train or employ alternative dental health care providers (e.g., community dental health coordinators, dental health aides) to increase access to dental health care services in rural and other underserved communities. Eligible grantees include institutions of higher education; public-private entities; FQHCs; facilities operated by the IHS or by Indian tribes or organizations; state or county public health clinics; public hospitals or health systems; and accredited dental education programs. | SSAN (no years specified). *FY2013 request = $1 million.* Note: The Consolidated Appropriations Act, 2012 (P.L. 112-74) prohibited HRSA funding for this new program in FY2012. |

| ACA Section | Statutory Authority (Agency) | Summary of Provision | Authorization of Appropriations; Funding (FY2011-FY2013) |
|---|---|---|---|
| **Nursing: Existing Programs** | | | |
| 5309(a) | Amends and reauthorizes PHSA Sec. 831 (HRSA) | **Nurse education, practice, quality, and retention program.** Authorizes grants or contracts to expand enrollment in baccalaureate nursing programs; provide training in new technologies; develop cultural competencies; expand nursing practice arrangements in non-institutional settings; and support nurse retention programs that offer career advancement for nursing personnel, enhance collaboration among nurses and other health professionals, and promote nurse involvement in clinical decision making. Eligible grantees include nursing schools, health care facilities (including NMHCs), or partnerships of the two. | SSAN for each of FY2010 through FY2014. See also ACA Sec. 5312 below, which reauthorized appropriations for several Title VIII nursing education programs, including Sec. 831.<br><br>*FY2011 funding = $40 million, FY2012 funding = $39 million, FY2013 request = $39 million.* [CFDA 93.359, 93.503] |
| 5311(a) | Amends and reauthorizes PHSA Sec. 846A (HRSA) | **Nursing faculty loan program.** Authorizes loans to nursing school students pursuing advanced degrees to become qualified nursing faculty. Sets the annual loan limit at $35,500 for FY2010 and FY2011; for subsequent fiscal years, the loan limit is subject to a cost-of-attendance adjustment. Students who go on to serve as nursing school faculty may have up to 85% of their loan repayment cancelled. | SSAN for each of FY2010 through FY2014.<br><br>*FY2011 funding = $25 million, FY2012 funding = $25 million, FY2013 request = $25 million.* [CFDA 93.264] |
| 5312 | Amends PHSA Sec. 871; previously Sec. 841 (HRSA) | **Authorization of appropriations.** Reauthorizes funding for the following PHSA Title VIII nursing workforce programs:<br><br>1. Advanced nursing education (PHSA Sec. 811) – grants to accredited programs for advanced nurse education including combined registered nurse masters degree programs, authorized nurse practitioner programs, accredited nurse midwifery programs, and accredited nurse anesthesia programs.<br><br>2. Nursing workforce diversity (PHSA Sec. 821) – grants to nursing schools, academic health centers, state or local governments, and other appropriate public or private nonprofit entities for stipends and scholarships so as to increase nursing education opportunities for disadvantaged individuals.<br><br>3. Nurse education, practice, quality, and retention (PHSA Sec. 831) – see ACA Sec. 5309(a) above.<br><br>Note: ACA did not reauthorize funding for the nursing education loan repayment and scholarship programs authorized under PHSA Sec. 846.[b] | For PHSA Secs. 811, 821, 831, and new 831A (see ACA Sec. 5309(b) below), $338 million for FY2010, and SSAN for each of FY2011 through FY2016.<br><br>*Sec. 811: FY2011 funding = $64 million, FY2012 funding = $64 million, FY2013 request = $84 million (includes $20 million in PHS evaluation funds).*[a] [CFDA 93.124, 93.247, 93.358, 93.513]<br><br>*Sec. 821: FY2011 funding = $16 million, FY2012 funding = $16 million, FY2013 request = $16 million.* [CFDA 93.178]<br><br>*Sec. 831: see ACA Sec. 5309(a) above for funding amounts.* |

| ACA Section | Statutory Authority (Agency) | Summary of Provision | Authorization of Appropriations; Funding (FY2011-FY2013) |
|---|---|---|---|
| **Nursing: New Programs** | | | |
| 5309(b) | New PHSA Sec. 831A (HRSA) | **Nurse retention program.** New authority that largely duplicates the nurse retention grant program authorized under PHSA Sec. 831; see ACA Sec. 5309(a) above. | SSAN for each of FY2010 through FY2012. See also ACA Sec. 5312 above. |
| 5311(b) | New PHSA Sec. 847 (HRSA) | **Nursing faculty loan repayment program.** Authorizes a loan repayment program for qualified nursing students or graduates who agree to serve as nursing faculty for four to six years. Sets the annual loan limit for FY2010 and FY2011 at $10,000 for individuals with a master's or equivalent degree in nursing ($20,000 for those with a doctorate or equivalent degree in nursing), and an aggregate loan limit of $40,000 for individuals with a master's or equivalent degree in nursing ($80,000 for those with a doctorate or equivalent degree in nursing). Thereafter, the annual and aggregate loan limits are subject to a cost-of-attendance adjustment. | SSAN for each of FY2010 through FY2014. |
| 5316 | New authority | **Family nurse practitioner demonstration program.** Requires the Secretary to award three-year demonstration grants to FQHCs and NMHCs, not to exceed $600,000 a year, for programs to train nurse practitioners as primary care providers (as defined in ACA Sec. 5208). Preference given to bilingual individuals. | SSAN for each of FY2011 through FY2014. |
| **Geriatrics and Long-Term Care: Existing Program** | | | |
| 5305(c) | Amends and reauthorizes PHSA Sec. 865; previously Sec. 855 (HRSA) | **Geriatric nursing education and training.** Provides grants for traineeships for individuals preparing for advanced degrees in geriatric nursing or other nursing areas that specialize in elder care. Eligible grantees include nursing schools, health care facilities, programs leading to certification as a certified nurse assistant, and partnerships of such schools, facilities, and programs. | SSAN for each of FY2010 through FY2014. *FY2011 funding = $5 million, FY2012 funding = $4 million, FY2013 request = $4 million.* [CFDA 93.265] |
| **Geriatrics and Long-Term Care (LTC): New Programs** | | | |
| 5302 | New PHSA Sec. 747A (HRSA) | **Direct care worker training.** Requires the Secretary to establish a grant program to provide new training opportunities, such as tuition and fee assistance, for direct care workers employed in LTC settings. Individuals who receive assistance are required to work in the field of geriatrics, disability services, LTC services and supports, or chronic care management for a minimum of two years. Eligible grantees include institutions of higher education that have an established partnership with an LTC entity, as specified. | $10 million for the period FY2011 through FY2013. |

| ACA Section | Statutory Authority (Agency) | Summary of Provision | Authorization of Appropriations; Funding (FY2011-FY2013) |
|---|---|---|---|
| 5305(a) | Amends PHSA Sec. 753 by adding new subsections (d)-(e) (HRSA) | **Geriatric workforce development; geriatric career incentive awards.** (1) Requires the Secretary to award no more than 24 grants or contracts for $150,000 to entities that operate geriatric education centers to support short-term intensive courses on geriatrics and LTC, and support training for family caregivers and direct care workers. Eligible grantees include accredited schools of allied health, medicine, nursing, dentistry, osteopathic medicine, optometry, podiatric medicine, veterinary medicine, public health, or chiropractic care; accredited graduate programs in clinical psychology, clinical social work, health administration, marriage and family therapy, and counseling; and physician assistant programs. (2) Requires the Secretary to award grants or contracts to advance practice nurses, clinical social workers, pharmacists, and psychologists pursuing an advanced degree in geriatrics or a related field, in return for agreeing to teach or practice in the field of geriatrics, LTC, or chronic care management for a minimum of five years upon completion of the degree. | (1) $10.8 million for the period FY2011 through FY2014. (2) $10 million for the period FY2011 through FY2013. Note: Funding for the three existing geriatric education and training programs under PHSA Sec. 753(a)-(c) is as follows: FY2011 funding = $34 million; FY2012 funding = $31 million, FY2013 request = $31 million. [CFDA 93.156, 93.250, 93.969] |
| **Pain Care: New Program** | | | |
| 4305(c) | New PHSA Sec. 759 (HRSA) | **Education and training in pain care.** Authorizes a grant program to train health professionals in pain care. Eligible grantees include health professions schools, hospices, and other public and private entities. Applicants must agree to include training and education on recognizing the signs and symptoms of pain; applicable laws and policies on controlled substances; interdisciplinary approaches to pain care delivery; barriers to care in underserved populations; and recent developments in pain care. [See also **Table 14**.] | SSAN for each of FY2010 through FY2012, to remain available until expended. |
| **Public Health: Existing Programs** | | | |
| 10501(m)(2) | Amends PHSA Sec. 770 (HRSA) | **Public health and preventive medicine programs.** Reauthorizes funding for the public health workforce programs authorized under PHSA Secs. 765-769. They include grants for public health training centers; tuition, fees, and stipends for traineeships in public health and in health administration; and residency programs in preventive medicine and dental public health. Several programs mention preference for underserved communities or underrepresented minorities. Eligible grantees include accredited academic institutions, as well as state, local and tribal public health departments. | $43 million for FY2011, and SSAN for each of FY2012 through FY2015. *FY2011 funding = $30 million (includes $20 million from the PPHF), FY2012 funding = $33 million (includes $25 million from the PPHF), FY2013 request = $20 million (includes $10 million from the PPHF).* [CFDA 93.117, 93.249, 93.516, 93.964] |

| ACA Section | Statutory Authority (Agency) | Summary of Provision | Authorization of Appropriations; Funding (FY2011-FY2013) |
|---|---|---|---|
| **Public Health: New Programs** | | | |
| 5204 | New PHSA Sec. 776 (HRSA) | **Public health workforce loan repayment program.** Requires the Secretary to establish a student loan repayment program that pays up to $35,000 a year, or one-third of total debt, whichever is less, to increase the supply of public health professionals. Eligible individuals must agree to work for at least three years in a public health agency or related training fellowship. | $195 million for FY2010, and SSAN for each of FY2011 through FY2015. |
| 5206(b) | New PHSA Sec. 777 (HRSA) | **Public health and allied health scholarship program.** Authorizes grants to accredited institutions for scholarships to help support the training of mid-career professionals in public health and allied health. Available grant funds are to be divided 50:50 between supporting public health and allied health professionals. | $60 million for FY2010, and SSAN for each of FY2011 through FY2015. |
| 5313 | New PHSA Sec. 399V (CDC) | **Community health worker (CHW) program.** Requires CDC to award grants to promote healthy behaviors and outcomes for populations in medically underserved communities through programs of training and supervision of CHWs. Eligible grantees include states and subdivisions, health departments, free clinics, hospitals, and FQHCs. Priority is to be given to applicants that target areas with a high proportion of uninsured or underinsured individuals, or with high rates of chronic illness or infant mortality. | SSAN for each of FY2010 through FY2014. |
| 5314 | New PHSA Sec. 778 (CDC) | **CDC training fellowships.** Authorizes the Secretary to expand existing CDC training fellowships in epidemiology, laboratory science, and informatics; the Epidemic Intelligence Service (EIS); and other training programs that meet similar objectives. Participants may be placed in state and local health agencies, and states can receive federal assistance for loan repayment programs for such participants. [CFDA 93.065] | $39.5 million for each of FY2010 through FY2013 ($24.5 million for EIS, and $5 million each for epidemiology, laboratory science, and informatics). |
| 5315 | New PHSA Title II, Part D – Secs. 271-274 (U.S. Surgeon General) | **United States Public Health Sciences Track.** Authorizes the establishment of a science track at academic sites selected by the Secretary to award degrees that emphasize team-based service, public health, epidemiology, and emergency preparedness and response. Funds may be used for program development and for tuition and stipends for student who meet a service obligation, including in the United States Public Health Service (USPHS) Commissioned Corps. | Requires the Secretary to transfer SSAN from the Public Health and Social Services Emergency Fund for FY2010 and each fiscal year thereafter. Note: P.L. 112-10 prohibited any such transfer of funds.[c] |

| ACA Section | Statutory Authority (Agency) | Summary of Provision | Authorization of Appropriations; Funding (FY2011-FY2013) |
|---|---|---|---|
| 5210 | Amends PHSA Sec. 203 (U.S. Surgeon General) | **USPHS Commissioned Corps.** Establishes a Ready Reserve Corps of officers who are subject to involuntary call to active duty (including for training) by the Surgeon General, in order to bolster the available workforce for both routine and emergency public health missions. | $17.5 million for each of FY2010 through FY2014 ($5 million for recruitment and training, $12.5 million for the Ready Reserve Corps). |

**Workforce Diversity, Health Disparities, Cultural Competency: Existing Programs**

| ACA Section | Statutory Authority (Agency) | Summary of Provision | Authorization of Appropriations; Funding (FY2011-FY2013) |
|---|---|---|---|
| 5307(a) | Amends and reauthorizes PHSA Sec. 741 (HRSA) | **Cultural competency, prevention, public health, disparities, and individuals with disability training.** Authorizes grants, contracts, or cooperative agreements under PHSA Title VII (Health Professions Education) for the development and evaluation of research, demonstration projects, and model curricula that provide training in cultural competency, prevention, public health proficiency, reducing health disparities, and aptitude for working with individuals with disabilities. The Secretary is required to coordinate this program with the one authorized under PHSA Sec. 807. | SSAN for each of FY2010 through FY2015. |
| 5307(b) | Amends and reauthorizes PHSA Sec. 807 (HRSA) | **Cultural competency, prevention, public health, disparities, and individuals with disability training.** Authorizes grants, contracts, or cooperative agreements under PHSA Title VIII (Nursing Workforce Development) for the development and evaluation of research, demonstration projects, and model curricula that provide training in cultural competency, prevention, public health proficiency, reducing health disparities, and aptitude for working with individuals with disabilities. The Secretary is required to coordinate this program with the one authorized under PHSA Sec. 741. | SSAN for each of FY2010 through FY2015. |
| 5401 | Amends and reauthorizes PHSA Sec. 736 (HRSA) | **Centers of excellence (COE).** Requires the Secretary to fund COEs at health professions schools that recruit, enroll and graduate underrepresented minorities or that recruit underrepresented minorities serving in faculty or administrative positions. | $50 million for each of FY2010 through FY2015, and SSAN for each subsequent fiscal year.<br><br>*FY2011 funding = $24 million, FY2012 funding = $23 million, FY2013 request = $23 million.* [CFDA 93.157] |

| ACA Section | Statutory Authority (Agency) | Summary of Provision | Authorization of Appropriations; Funding (FY2011-FY2013) |
|---|---|---|---|
| 5402 | Amends PHSA Sec. 740 (HRSA) | **Authorization of appropriations.** Reauthorizes funding for the following PHSA Title VII workforce diversity programs:<br><br>1.   Scholarships for disadvantaged students (PHSA Sec. 737) – grants to health professions schools for awarding scholarships to students from disadvantaged backgrounds with financial need.<br><br>2.   Faculty loan repayment program (PHSA Sec. 738) – loan repayment program for health profession graduates from disadvantaged backgrounds who serve as faculty at an eligible health professions college for at least two years.<br><br>3.   Health careers opportunity program (PHSA Sec. 739) – grants to health professions schools and other educational institutions to improve recruitment and academic preparation of students from disadvantaged backgrounds. | For Sec. 737, $51 million for FY2010, and SSAN for each of FY2011 through FY2014. For Sec. 738, $5 million for each of FY2010 through FY2014. For Sec. 739, $60 million for FY2010, and SSAN for each of FY2011 through FY2014.<br><br>*Sec. 737: FY2011 funding = $49 million, FY2012 funding = $47 million, FY2013 request = $47. [CFDA 93.925]*<br><br>*Sec. 738: FY2011 funding = $1 million, FY2012 funding = $1 million, FY2013 request = $1 million. [CFDA 93.923]*<br><br>*Sec. 739: FY2011 funding = $22 million, FY2012 funding = $15 million, FY2013 request = $0. [CFDA 93.822]* |
| 5403(a) | Amends and reauthorizes PHSA Sec. 751 (HRSA) | **Area Health Education Centers (AHECs).** Requires the Secretary to award grants (with a matching requirement) to medical and nursing schools of at least $250,000 to (1) plan, develop, and operate AHEC programs; and (2) to maintain and improve the effectiveness of existing AHEC programs. AHECs recruit, train, and prepare individuals from minority populations or from disadvantaged or rural backgrounds to work in medically underserved areas. | $125 million for each of FY2010 through FY2014; funds may be carried over for up to three fiscal years.<br><br>*FY2011 funding = $33 million, FY2012 funding = $27 million, FY2013 request = $0. [CFDA 93.107, 93.824]* |
| **Workforce Diversity, Health Disparities, Cultural Competency: New Program** | | | |
| 5403(b) | New PHSA Sec. 752 (HRSA) | **Continuing educational support for health professionals serving in underserved communities.** Requires the Secretary to award grants to enhance education through distance learning, continuing education, collaborative conferences, and telehealth, with a focus on primary care. Eligible grantees include health professions schools, academic health centers, state or local governments, or other public or nonprofit entities participating in training activities. [CFDA 93.189] | $5 million for each of FY2010 through FY2014, and SSAN for each subsequent fiscal year. |

| ACA Section | Statutory Authority (Agency) | Summary of Provision | Authorization of Appropriations; Funding (FY2011-FY2013) |
|---|---|---|---|
| **Mental and Behavioral Health: New Program** | | | |
| 5306 | Redesignates PHSA Sec. 756 as Sec. 757, and adds a new Sec. 756 (HRSA) | **Mental and behavioral health education and training grants.** Authorizes grants for the recruitment and education of students in social work, interdisciplinary psychology training, and internships or other field placement programs related to child and adolescent mental health. Priority for social work grants given to schools of social work meeting certain criteria such as recruiting from and placing graduates into areas with a high-need and high-demand population. Priority for psychology grants given to institutions that focus on the needs of specified vulnerable groups. Priority for grants to train professional and paraprofessional child and adolescent mental health workers given to applicants that can, among other things, assess workforce needs and that have programs designed to increase the number of child and adolescent mental health workers serving high-priority populations. | $35 million for the period of FY2010 through FY2013 ($8 million for training in social work, $12 million for training in graduate psychology, $10 million for training in professional child and adolescent mental health, and $5 million for training in paraprofessional child and adolescent mental health). *FY2012 funding = $10 million from the PPHF, FY2013 request = $5 million in PHS evaluation funds.*[a] [CFDA 93.732] Note: The existing graduate psychology education program received $3 million in FY2011 and in FY2012; the FY2013 request is for the same amount. |
| **Policy and Planning: Existing Program** | | | |
| 5103 | Amends and reauthorizes PHSA Sec. 761 (HRSA) | **Health care workforce program assessment.** Requires the Secretary to establish a National Center for Health Care Workforce Analysis, award grants to support state and regional centers for health workforce analysis, and increase funding for longitudinal evaluations of specified individuals who have received education, training, or financial assistance from programs under PHSA Title VII. | For the National Center, $7.5 million for each of FY2010 through FY2014; for state and regional centers, $4.5 million for each of FY2010 through FY2014; and for longitudinal evaluations, SSAN for FY2010 through FY2014. *FY2011 funding = $3 million, FY2012 funding = $3 million, FY2013 request = $10 million.* Note: Includes funding for Sec. 792 (health professions data) and Sec. 806 (nursing grant program data). FY2013 request is all PHS evaluation funds.[a] [CFDA 93.300] |
| **Policy and Planning: New Programs** | | | |
| 5101 | New authority | **National Health Care Workforce Commission.** Establishes a 15-member commission focused on evaluating and meeting the need for health care workers in the United States. The commission is required to conduct studies, produce annual reports beginning in 2011, and make recommendations on high-priority topics related to the health care workforce. | SSAN (no years specified). |

| ACA Section | Statutory Authority (Agency) | Summary of Provision | Authorization of Appropriations; Funding (FY2011-FY2013) |
|---|---|---|---|
| 5102 | New authority (HRSA) | **State health care workforce development grants.** Establishes a matching grants program for state partnerships to plan and implement activities leading to coherent and comprehensive health care workforce development strategies at the state and local levels. Planning grants of up to $150,000 are for up to one year and require a 15% match. Implementation grants are for up to two years (with up to one additional year of funding) and require a 25% match. | For planning grants, $8 million for FY2010, and SSAN for each subsequent fiscal year. For implementation grants, $150 million for FY2010, and SSAN for each subsequent fiscal year. Note: This program received $6 million in FY2010 funds from the PPHF. [CFDA 93.509] |

**Sources:** Table prepared by the Congressional Research Service based on the text of the Patient Protection and Affordable Care Act (ACA; P.L. 111-148, as amended). FY2011, FY2012 and requested FY2013 funding amounts are taken from HHS agency FY2013 congressional justification documents, available at http://www.hrsa.gov/about/budget/index.html.

a. PHSA Sec. 241 authorizes the Secretary to use a portion of the funds appropriated for PHSA programs to evaluate their implementation and effectiveness. Under this authority a number of HHS agencies and offices are subject to a budget tap, called the PHS Program Evaluation Set-Aside. The tapped evaluation funds are redistributed and used for evaluation and other specific programs within HHS.

b. The nursing education loan repayment program repays 60% of a registered nurse's educational loans in return for a two-year commitment to work in a health care facility with a critical shortage of nurses. Participants may have an additional 25% of their loan repaid in exchange for one more year of service. The nurse scholarship program offer scholarships to individuals attending nursing school in exchange for at least two years working in a health care facility with a critical shortage of nurses. Together the two programs, authorized under PHSA Sec. 846, received $94 million in FY2010 and $93 million in FY2011. The authorization of appropriations for Sec. 846 expired at the end of FY2007 and was not reauthorized by ACA.

c. The Department of Defense and Full-Year Continuing Appropriations Act, 2011 (P.L. 112-10, Div. B, Sec. 1828) prohibited the transfer of funds from the Public Health and Social Services Emergency Fund (PHSSEF) to support the U.S. Public Health Sciences Track. The PHSSEF is an HHS account administered by the Secretary. Congress has historically used the PHSSEF to provide one-time funding for non-routine activities. Each fiscal year, Congress appropriates amounts to the PHSSEF for specified purposes. ACA did not authorize or appropriate funds to the PHSSEF.

## Table 3. ACA Discretionary Spending: Prevention and Wellness

| ACA Section | Statutory Authority (Agency) | Summary of Provision | Authorization of Appropriations; Funding (FY2011-FY2013) |
|---|---|---|---|
| **Community-Based Prevention: Existing Programs** | | | |
| 3509/3511 | New PHSA Secs. 229 (OS), 310A (CDC), 925 (AHRQ); new SSA Sec. 713 (HRSA); and new FFDCA Sec. 1011 (FDA). Reauthorizes PHSA Secs. 486(a) (NIH) and 501(f) (SAMHSA). | **Offices on Women's Health.** Establishes or reauthorizes offices of women's health in OS, CDC, AHRQ, HRSA, FDA, NIH, and SAMHSA. Grants, agreements, or contracts may be awarded for activities of the OS office to establish an information center and coordinating committee. Activities of other offices include recommendations regarding grant-making through other agency accounts, not direct grant-making. | For most offices, SSAN for each of FY2010 through FY2014. For NIH and SAMHSA offices, SSAN (no years specified). *OS Office on Women's Health: FY2011 funding = $34 million, FY2012 funding = $34 million, FY2013 request = $29 million.* *NIH Office of Research on Women's Health: FY2011 funding = $42 million, FY2012 funding = $42 million, FY2013 request = $42 million.* |
| 4003 | Amends PHSA Sec. 915(a) (AHRQ). New PHSA Sec. 399U (CDC). | **Clinical and community preventive services task forces.** Reauthorizes and expands the authority for the U.S. Preventive Services Task Force (USPSTF) to review and recommend effective clinical preventive services. Provides explicit statutory authority for the existing Task Force on Community Preventive Services (TFCPS) to review and recommend effective community-based interventions. | SSAN for each fiscal year to carry out the activities of the USPSTF and the TFCPS. *USPSTF: Funding for each of FY2011, FY2012, and the FY2013 request = $11 million (includes $7 million from the PPHF).* |
| 4102(b) | Amends PHSA Sec. 317M(c) (CDC, HRSA) | **School-based dental sealant program.** Amends the existing school-based dental sealant grant program, which was discretionary, by requiring the Secretary to award grants to the 50 states and to Indian tribes for school-based dental sealant programs. | Authority expired at end of FY2005; ACA does not authorize new funding. *Funding for all CDC's existing oral health programs under Sec. 317M: FY2011 = $15 million; FY2012 = $15 million, FY2013 request = $15 million.* |
| 4204 | Amends PHSA Sec. 317 and adds a new subsection (m) (CDC) | **Immunization programs.** Provides explicit authority for states to purchase vaccines at prices negotiated by Secretary. Permanently reauthorizes state immunization grants. Requires new immunization demonstration grants. | SSAN for each of FY2010 through FY2014 for demonstration grants; SSAN (no years specified) for other authorities. *Funding for the Sec. 317 vaccination program: FY2011 = $589 million (includes $100 million from the PPHF), FY2012 = $620 million (includes $190 million from the PPHF), FY2013 request = $562 million (includes $72 million from the PPHF). [CFDA 93.185, 93.268, 93.533, 93.539]* |

| ACA Section | Statutory Authority (Agency) | Summary of Provision | Authorization of Appropriations; Funding (FY2011-FY2013) |
|---|---|---|---|
| 10334 | Amends PHSA Sec. 1707 (OS) and PHSA Title IV (NIH) | **Offices of Minority Health.** Elevates the existing OS Office of Minority Health and NIH National Center on Minority Health and Health Disparities (NCMHD); instructs the OS office to award grants and undertake other activities to improve minority health status; and gives the new NIH National Institute on Minority Health and Health Disparities (NIMHD) responsibility for minority health disparities research and other health disparities research at NIH. | SSAN for each of FY2011 through FY2016 for OS office.

*NIMHD: FY2011 funding = $276 million, FY2012 funding = $276 million, FY2013 request = $279 million.*

*OS Office of Minority Health: FY2011 funding = $56 million, FY2012 funding = $56 million, FY2013 request = $41 million.* |
| 10412 | Reauthorizes PHSA Sec. 312 (HRSA) | **Rural access to emergency devices.** Reauthorizes a program of grants to community partnerships for the purchase and distribution of automatic external defibrillators (AEDs) in rural communities, and to support AED training for first responders. | $25 million for each of FY2003 through FY2014.

*FY2011 funding = $236,000, FY2012 funding = $1 million, FY2013 request = $0.* [CFDA 93.259] |
| **Community-Based Prevention: New Programs** | | | |
| 4004 | New authority | **Education and outreach regarding prevention.** Requires the Secretary to carry out various specified communications activities regarding health promotion and disease prevention, for common and serious chronic health problems. They include establishing, within one year of enactment, a national media campaign on health promotion and disease prevention. | SSAN for each fiscal year; no more than $500 million total. |
| 4102(a) | New PHSA Secs. 399LL, 399LL-1, and 399LL-2 (CDC) | **Oral health activities.** Requires CDC, subject to appropriations, to fund a five-year national oral health education campaign, and award grants to community-based providers of dental services for dental caries disease management programs, among other things. | SSAN (no years specified). |
| 4102(c) | Amends PHSA Sec. 317M by adding a new subsection (d) (CDC) | **Oral health infrastructure.** Requires the Secretary to enter into cooperative agreements with states and tribal entities to establish oral health leadership and programs to improve oral health. | SSAN for FY2010 through FY2014. |
| 4102(d) | New authority (CDC, AHRQ) | **Oral health surveillance.** Requires the Secretary to expand the following surveillance systems to include more information on oral health: Pregnancy Risk Assessment Monitoring System (PRAMS); National Health and Nutrition Examination Survey (NHANES); National Oral Health Surveillance System (NOHSS); and Medical Expenditure Panel Survey (MEPS). | SSAN (no years specified) for PRAMS; SSAN for each of FY2010 through FY2014 for NOHSS; no explicit authorization of appropriations for NHANES/MEPS expansion. |

| ACA Section | Statutory Authority (Agency) | Summary of Provision | Authorization of Appropriations; Funding (FY2011-FY2013) |
|---|---|---|---|
| 4201 | New authority (CDC) | **Community transformation grants.** Requires CDC to fund competitive grants for the implementation, evaluation, and dissemination of evidence-based community preventive health activities. | SSAN for each of FY2010 through FY2014.<br><br>*FY2011 funding = $145 million, FY2012 funding = $226 million, FY2013 request = $146 million; all funds are from the PPHF.* [CFDA 93.531] |
| 4202(a) | New authority (CDC) | **Community wellness pilot program.** Requires CDC to award grants state and local health departments, and to Indian tribes, for five-year pilot programs to provide community prevention interventions, screenings, and clinical referrals for individuals between 55 and 64 years of age. | SSAN for each of FY2010 through FY2014. |
| 4206 | Amends PHSA Sec. 330 by adding a new subsection (s) | **Individualized wellness plan demonstration program.** Requires the Secretary to establish a pilot program in not more than 10 community health centers to test the impact of providing at-risk individuals who use the centers with individualized wellness plans. | SSAN (no years specified). |
| 4304 | New PHSA Sec. 2821 (CDC) | **Epidemiology and laboratory capacity grants.** Codifies existing grant program to strengthen national epidemiology, laboratory, and information management capacity for the response to infectious diseases and other conditions of public health importance. | $190 million for each of FY2010 through FY2013 (at least $95 million for epidemiology, $60 million for information management, and $32 million for laboratories). |
| 10407 | New authority (CDC) | **Diabetes activities.** Requires CDC to conduct several diabetes prevention activities including state assessments, vital statistics, physician education, and funding of an Institute of Medicine (IOM) report. | SSAN (no years specified). |
| 10411 | New PHSA Secs. 399V-2 (CDC) and 425 (NIH) | **Congenital heart disease programs.** Authorizes CDC to establish a National Congenital Heart Disease Surveillance System (NCHDSS), or to award one grant to establish such a system. Authorizes NIH to expand and coordinate research on congenital heart disease. | SSAN for each of FY2011 through FY2015 for both the surveillance system and the expanded research program. |
| 10413 | New PHSA Sec. 399NN (OS, CDC) | **Young women's breast health awareness.** Among other things, requires CDC to conduct an education campaign and award grants for a media campaign regarding breast health in young women, and to conduct prevention research; requires the Secretary to award grants to provide education and assistance to young women diagnosed with breast disease. | $9 million for each of FY2010 through FY2014. |
| 10501(g) | New PHSA Sec. 399V-3 (CDC) | **National diabetes prevention program.** Among other things, requires the Secretary to award grants for community-based diabetes prevention program model sites. | SSAN for each of FY2010 through FY2014. |

| ACA Section | Statutory Authority (Agency) | Summary of Provision | Authorization of Appropriations; Funding (FY2011-FY2013) |
|---|---|---|---|
| **Workplace Wellness: New Program** | | | |
| 10408 | New authority (CDC) | **Small business wellness program.** Requires the Secretary to award grants to employers to provide their employees with access to comprehensive workplace wellness programs. Eligible employers are those with fewer than 100 employees, who work at least 25 hours per week. | $200 million for the period of FY2011 through FY2015, to remain available until expended.<br><br>*FY2011 funding = $10 million, FY2012 funding = $10 million, FY2013 request = $4 million; all funds are from the PPHF.* |

**Sources:** Table prepared by the Congressional Research Service based on the text of the Patient Protection and Affordable Care Act (ACA; P.L. 111-148, as amended). FY2011, FY2012 and requested FY2013 funding amounts are taken from PHS agency FY2013 congressional justification documents, available at http://www.hrsa.gov/about/budget/index.html.

## Table 4. ACA Discretionary Spending: Maternal and Child Health

| ACA Section | Statutory Authority (Agency) | Summary of Provision | Authorization of Appropriations; Funding (FY2011-FY2013) |
|---|---|---|---|
| 2952(b) | New SSA Sec. 512 (HRSA) | **Services to individuals with a postpartum condition.** Authorizes grants to establish, operate and coordinate effective and cost-efficient systems for the delivery of essential services to individuals with, or at risk of, postpartum depression and their families. Eligible grantees include public or nonprofit private entities, state or local government public-private partnerships, recipients of Healthy Start grants, public or nonprofit private hospitals, community-based organizations, hospices, ambulatory care facilities, community health centers, and primary care centers. | $3 million for FY2010, and SSAN for each of FY2011 and FY2012. |

**Source:** Table prepared by the Congressional Research Service based on the text of the Patient Protection and Affordable Care Act (ACA; P.L. 111-148, as amended).

## Table 5. ACA Discretionary Spending: Health Care Quality

| ACA Section | Statutory Authority (Agency) | Summary of Provision | Authorization of Appropriations; Funding (FY2011-FY2013) |
|---|---|---|---|
| **Quality Measure Development, Analysis, and Public Reporting: New Programs** | | | |
| 3013(a)&(c) | New PHSA 931 (AHRQ) | **Quality measure development.** Requires the Secretary, in consultation with AHRQ and CMS, to (1) identify gaps where no quality measures exist or where existing measures need improvement, updating or expansion consistent with the National Strategy for Quality Improvement; and (2) fund or enter into agreements with eligible entities that have demonstrated expertise in measure development to develop, improve, update or expand quality measures in areas identified as gap areas. | $75 million for each of FY2010 through FY2014, to remain available until expended. At least 50% of the amounts appropriated must be used pursuant to SSA Sec. 1890A(e), as added by ACA Sec. 3013(b). See below. |
| 3013(b) | Amends new SSA Sec. 1890A, as added by ACA Sec. 3014(b), by adding a new subsection (e) (CMS) | **Quality and efficiency measures development.** Requires CMS, in consultation with AHRQ, through contracts, to develop quality and efficiency measures as determined appropriate for use under the SSA. | See ACA Sec. 3013(a)&(c) above. |
| 3015 | New PHSA Sec. 399II | **Collection and analysis of data for quality and resource use measures.** Requires the Secretary to establish and implement an overall strategic framework to carry out the public reporting of performance information. Requires the Secretary to collect and aggregate consistent data on quality and resource use measures, and authorizes the Secretary to award grants or contracts for this purpose. Authorizes the Secretary to award grants or contracts to multi-stakeholder entities to support new, or improve existing, efforts to collect and aggregate quality and resource use measures. | SSAN for each of FY2010 through FY2014. |
| 3015 | New PHSA Sec. 399JJ | **Public reporting of performance information.** Requires the Secretary to make available to the public, through standardized websites, performance information summarizing data on quality measures. The information must include clinical conditions to the extent such data is available and, where appropriate, be provider-specific and sufficiently disaggregated and specific to meet the needs of patients with different clinical conditions. | SSAN for each of FY2010 through FY2014. |

| ACA Section | Statutory Authority (Agency) | Summary of Provision | Authorization of Appropriations; Funding (FY2011-FY2013) |
|---|---|---|---|
| **Quality Improvement Research, Training, and Implementation: New Programs** | | | |
| 3501 | New PHSA Sec. 933 (AHRQ) | **Health care delivery system research.** Requires AHRQ to (1) identify, develop, evaluate, and disseminate innovative strategies for quality improvement practices in the delivery of health care services that represent best practice; (2) support research on health care delivery improvement and facilitate adoption of best practices; and (3) make the research findings available to the public; among other specified functions. | $20 million for FY2010 through FY2014. |
| 3501/3511 | New PHSA Sec. 934 (AHRQ) | **Quality improvement technical assistance and implementation.** Requires AHRQ to award grants (with a matching requirement) to eligible entities for providing technical support to health care providers in order to help them understand, adapt, and implement the models and practices identified by the research conducted by the agency. Grantees must have demonstrated expertise in providing information and technical support and assistance to health care providers regarding quality improvement. | SSAN (no years specified). |
| 3508/3511 | New authority | **Quality and patient safety training.** Authorizes the Secretary to award demonstration grants (with a matching requirement) to eligible health professions schools or consortia to develop and implement academic curricula that integrate quality improvement and patient safety into clinical education of health professionals. | SSAN (no years specified). |
| **Health Care Coordination: Existing Program** | | | |
| 3510 | Amends and reauthorizes PHSA Sec. 340A (HRSA) | **Patient navigator program.** Prohibits the Secretary from awarding a grant to an entity under this section unless the entity provides assurances that patient navigators recruited, assigned, trained, or employed using these grant funds meet certain minimum core proficiencies. Eligible grantees include public or nonprofit private health centers (including an FQHCs), IHS facilities, hospitals, cancer centers, rural health clinics, academic health centers, and nonprofit entities that partner or coordinate referrals with such a facility to provide patient navigator services. | $3.5 million for FY2010, and SSAN for each of FY2011 through FY2015. *FY2011 funding = $5 million, FY2012 funding = $0, FY2013 request = $0.* [CFDA 93.191] |

| ACA Section | Statutory Authority (Agency) | Summary of Provision | Authorization of Appropriations; Funding (FY2011-FY2013) |
|---|---|---|---|
| **Health Care Coordination: New Programs** | | | |
| 3502/3511 | New authority | **Community health team grants to support medical homes.** Requires the Secretary to award grants to or enter into contracts with states, state-designated entities, and tribal organizations to support community-based interdisciplinary, interprofessional health teams in assisting primary care practices. Funding must be used to establish the health teams and to provide capitated payments to the providers. | SSAN (no years specified). |
| 3503/3511 | New PHSA Sec. 935 (AHRQ) | **Medication therapy management (MTM) grants.** Requires the Secretary, not later than May 1, 2010, to provide grants to support MTM services provided by licensed pharmacists that are targeted at patients who take four or more prescribed medications, take high-risk medications, have two or more chronic diseases, or have undergone a transition of care or other factors that are likely to create a high risk for medication-related problems. | SSAN (no years specified). |
| 3506 | New PHSA Sec. 936 (AHRQ) | **Program to facilitate shared decision making.** Requires the Secretary, through a contract, to develop and identify standards for patient decision aids, to review patient decision aids, and develop a certification process for determining whether patient decision aids meet those standards. The contract is to be awarded to the entity that holds the contract under SSA Sec. 1890 (currently the National Quality Forum). Further requires the Secretary to (1) award grants or contracts to develop, update, and produce patient decision aids, to test such materials to ensure they are balanced and evidence-based, and to educate providers on their use; and (2) to award grants for establishing Shared Decision Making Resource Centers to develop and disseminate best practices to speed adoption and effective use of patient decision aids and shared decision making. Also requires the Secretary to award grants to providers for the development and implementation of shared decision-making techniques. | SSAN for FY2010 and each subsequent fiscal year. |

| ACA Section | Statutory Authority (Agency) | Summary of Provision | Authorization of Appropriations; Funding (FY2011-FY2013) |
|---|---|---|---|
| 5405 | New PHSA Sec. 399V-1 (AHRQ) | **Primary care extension program.** Requires the Secretary to establish a Primary Care Extension Program to award state planning and implementation grants for Primary Care Extension Program State Hubs, consisting of the state health department and other specified entities. State hubs must contract with and provide grant funds to county and local entities to serve as Primary Care Extension Agencies that assist primary care providers in implementing patient-centered medical homes and develop and support primary care learning communities, among other functions. | $120 million for each of FY2011 and FY2012, and SSAN for each of FY2013 and FY2014. |
| 5604 | New PHSA Sec. 520K (SAMHSA) | **Co-locating primary and specialty care in community-based mental health settings.** Requires the Secretary to fund demonstration projects for providing coordinated and integrated services to individuals with mental illness and co-occurring chronic diseases through the co-location of primary and specialty care services in community-based mental and behavioral health settings. | $50 million for FY2010, and SSAN for each of FY2011 through FY2014.<br><br>Note: SAMHSA's Primary & Behavioral Health Care Integration (PBHCI) program, authorized under PHSA Sec. 520A, predates ACA and has received the following amounts: FY2011 funding = $63 million (includes $35 million from the PPHF), FY2012 = $68 (includes $35 million from the PPHF), FY2013 request = $28 million (all PPHF). |
| 10333 | New PHSA Sec. 340H | **Community-based collaborative care network program.** Authorizes the Secretary to award grants to support community-based collaborative care networks (CCN). An eligible CCN is a consortium of health care providers with a joint governance structure that provides comprehensive coordinated and integrated health care services (as defined by the Secretary) for low-income populations. CCNs must include a safety net hospital and all FQHCs in the community, as specified. | SSAN for each of FY2011 through FY2015. |
| 10410 | New PHSA Sec. 520B (SAMHSA) | **Centers of excellence for depression.** Requires SAMHSA to award five-year grants (with a matching requirement) on a competitive basis to eligible institutions of higher education or research institutions to establish national centers of excellence for depression. One grantee is to be designated as the coordinating center and required to establish and maintain a national database. Centers of excellence may receive a grant of up to $5 million; the coordinating center may receive a grant of up to $10 million. | $100 million for each of FY2011 through FY2015, and $150 million for each of FY2016 through FY2020. |

**Sources:** Table prepared by the Congressional Research Service based on the text of the Patient Protection and Affordable Care Act (ACA; P.L. 111-148, as amended). FY2011, FY2012 and requested FY2013 funding amounts are taken from HHS agency FY2013 congressional justification documents, available at http://www.hrsa.gov/about/budget/index.html.

## Table 6. ACA Discretionary Spending: Nursing Homes

| ACA Section | Statutory Authority (Agency) | Summary of Provision | Authorization of Appropriations; Funding (FY2011-FY2013) |
|---|---|---|---|
| 6112 | New authority | **National independent monitor demonstration program.** Requires the Secretary, within one year of enactment, to implement a two-year demonstration to develop, test, and implement an independent monitoring program to oversee interstate and large intrastate chains of skilled nursing facilities (SNFs) and nursing facilities (NFs). | SSAN (no years specified); a monitored chain must contribute a portion of costs of the demonstration, as determined by the Secretary. |
| 6114 | New authority | **Culture change and information technology demonstration programs.** Requires the Secretary, within one year of enactment, to award one or more competitive grants to support each of the following two three-year demonstration projects for SNFs and NFs: (1) develop best practices for culture change (i.e., patient-centric models of care); and (2) develop best practices for the use of health information technology. | SSAN (no years specified). |

**Source:** Table prepared by the Congressional Research Service based on the text of the Patient Protection and Affordable Care Act (ACA; P.L. 111-148, as amended).

## Table 7. ACA Discretionary Spending: Health Disparities Data Collection

| ACA Section | Statutory Authority (Agency) | Summary of Provision | Authorization of Appropriations; Funding (FY2011-FY2013) |
|---|---|---|---|
| 4302(a) | New PHSA Title XXXI; new Sec. 3101 | **Health disparities data collection and analysis.** Not later than two years after enactment, requires federally conducted and supported health programs and surveys, to the extent practicable, to collect and report data on race, ethnicity, sex, primary language, and disability status, as well as other demographic data on health disparities as deemed appropriate by the Secretary. Requires the Secretary to adopt standards for the measurement and collection of such data. Requires the Secretary to analyze the data collected on health disparities; provide for the public reporting and dissemination of the data and analyses; and safeguard the privacy of the information. [Note: On October 31, 2011, HHS published final standards for collecting and reporting health disparities data. See http://minorityhealth.hhs.gov/templates/browse.aspx?lvl=2&lvlid=208.] | SSAN for each of FY2010 through FY2014; however, data may not be collected unless funds are directly appropriated for such purpose. |
| 5605 | New authority | **Key national indicators.** Establishes a Commission on Key National Indicators composed of eight members appointed by Congress. [Note: The Commission members were appointed in Dec. 2010. See http://www.stateoftheusa.org/content/commission-on-key-national-ind.php.] Requires the commission to contract with the National Academy of Sciences to review available public and private sector research on key national indicator set selection and determine how best to establish a key national indicator system, among other things. Mandates a Government Accountability Office (GAO) study of previous efforts by public, private, or foreign entities to develop best practices for a key national indicator system. [Note: GAO released its study in March 2011. See http://www.gao.gov/new.items/d11396.pdf.] | $10 million for FY2010, and $7.5 million for each of FY2011 through FY2018, with amounts appropriated to remain available until expended. |

**Source:** Table prepared by the Congressional Research Service based on the text of the Patient Protection and Affordable Care Act (ACA; P.L. 111-148, as amended).

## Table 8. ACA Discretionary Spending: Emergency Care and Trauma Services

| ACA Section | Statutory Authority (Agency) | Summary of Provision | Authorization of Appropriations; Funding (FY2011-FY2013) |
|---|---|---|---|
| **Emergency Care and Trauma Services: Existing Programs** | | | |
| 3505(a) | Amends and reauthorizes PHSA Secs. 1241-1245 (HRSA) | **Trauma care centers.** Requires the Secretary to establish separate grant programs for IHS and tribal trauma care centers to (1) help defray substantial uncompensated care costs, (2) further the core missions of trauma care centers, and (3) provide emergency relief to ensure the continued availability of trauma services. | $100 million for FY2009, and SSAN for each of FY2010 through FY2015. |
| 5603 | Amends and reauthorizes PHSA Sec. 1910 (HRSA) | **Children's emergency medical services demonstration grants.** Expands emergency services for children who need treatment for trauma or critical care by lengthening the period for demonstration grants to four years (with an optional fifth year). | $25 million for FY2010, $26.3 million for FY2011, $27.6 million for FY2012, $28.9 million for FY2013, and $30.4 million for FY2014. *FY2011 funding = $21 million, FY2012 funding = $21 million, FY2013 request = $21 million.* [CFDA 93.127] |
| **Emergency Care and Trauma Services: New Programs** | | | |
| 3504(a) | New PHSA Sec. 1204 (OS) | **Regional systems for emergency care.** Requires the Assistant Secretary for Preparedness and Response to award at least four multi-year contracts or grants (with matching requirement) to states and Indian tribes for pilot projects to improve regional coordination of emergency services. Priority given to entities that serve a medically underserved population. | $24 million for each of FY2010 through FY2014. Note: This provision reauthorized funding for several existing trauma care grant programs in PHSA Title XII Parts A and B (i.e., Secs. 1202, 1203, and 1211-1222), as well as for the new program (i.e., Sec. 1204). |
| 3504(b) | New PHSA Sec. 498D (NIH, AHRQ, HRSA, CDC) | **Emergency medicine research.** Requires the Secretary to expand and accelerate basic, translational, and service delivery research on emergency medical care systems and emergency medicine, including pediatric emergency medical care. Also requires the Secretary to support research on the economic impact of coordinated emergency care systems. | SSAN for each of FY2010 through FY2014. |
| 3505(b) | New PHSA Secs. 1281-1282 | **Trauma service availability grants.** Requires the Secretary to award grants to states for the purpose of supporting trauma-related physician specialties and broadening access to and availability of trauma care services. States must use at least 40% of the funds for grants to safety net trauma centers. | $100 million for each of FY2010 through FY2015. |

**Sources:** Table prepared by the Congressional Research Service based on the text of the Patient Protection and Affordable Care Act (ACA; P.L. 111-148, as amended). FY2011, FY2012 and requested FY2013 funding amounts are taken from HRSA's FY2013 congressional justification document, available at http://www.hrsa.gov/about/budget/index.html.

## Table 9. ACA Discretionary Spending: Elder Justice

| ACA Section | Statutory Authority (Agency) | Summary of Provision | Authorization of Appropriations; Funding (FY2011-FY2013) |
|---|---|---|---|
| 6703(a) | New SSA Sec. 2021 (OS) | **Elder Justice Coordinating Council.** Establishes an Elder Justice Coordinating Council to include the Secretary as chair and the U.S. Attorney General, as well as the head of each federal department or agency, identified by the chair, as having administrative responsibility or administering programs related to elder abuse, neglect, and exploitation. | SSAN (no years specified). See also new SSA Sec. 2024 below. |
| 6703(a) | New SSA Sec. 2022 | **Advisory Board on Elder Abuse, Neglect, and Exploitation.** Establishes an advisory board to create a short- and long-term multidisciplinary plan for development of the field of elder justice and to make recommendations to the Elder Justice Coordinating Council. | SSAN (no years specified). See also new SSA Sec. 2024 below. |
| 6703(a) | New SSA Sec. 2024 | **Authorization of appropriations.** Authorizes funding for new SSA Secs. 2021 (Coordinating Council), 2022 (Advisory Board), and 2023 (human subject protection guidelines for researchers). | $6.5 million for FY2011, and $7.0 million for each of FY2012 through FY2014. |
| 6703(a) | New SSA Sec. 2031 | **Forensic centers and expertise.** Requires the Secretary to award grants to eligible entities to establish and operate stationary and mobile forensic centers and to develop forensic expertise pertaining to elder abuse, neglect, and exploitation. | $4 million for FY2011, $6 million for FY2012, and $8 million for each of FY2013 and FY2014. |
| 6703(a) | New SSA Sec. 2041(a) | **Incentives for LTC staffing.** Requires the Secretary to award grants to LTC facilities for them to offer continuing training and varying levels of certification to employees providing direct care to residents, and to improve management practices so as to promote retention of direct care workers. | For new SSA Sec. 2041: $20 million for FY2011, $17.5 million for FY2012, and $15 million for each of FY2013 and FY2014. |
| 6703(a) | New SSA Sec. 2041(b) | **Certified EHR technology grant program.** Authorizes grants to LTC facilities for specified activities that would assist such entities in offsetting costs related to purchasing, leasing, developing and implementing certified electronic health record technology. | See above authorization of appropriations for SSA Sec. 2041. |
| 6703(a) | New SSA Sec. 2041(c) | **Standards for transactions involving clinical data by LTC facilities.** Requires the Secretary to adopt electronic standards for the exchange of clinical data by LTC facilities and, within 10 years, to have in place procedures to accept the optional electronic submission of clinical data by LTC facilities pursuant to such standards. | See above authorization of appropriations for SSA Sec. 2041. |
| 6703(a) | New SSA Sec. 2042(a) | **Adult protective service functions.** Requires the Secretary to undertake various activities with respect to adult protective services, including providing funding, collecting and disseminating data on elder abuse, disseminating information on best practices and training, conducting research, and providing technical assistance to states and other entities. | $3 million for FY2011, and $4 million for each of FY2012 through FY2014. |

*Discretionary Spending in the Patient Protection and Affordable Care Act (ACA)*

| ACA Section | Statutory Authority (Agency) | Summary of Provision | Authorization of Appropriations; Funding (FY2011-FY2013) |
|---|---|---|---|
| 6703(a) | New SSA Sec. 2042(b) | **Grants to enhance provision of adult protective services.** Requires the Secretary to award formula grants to states to enhance adult protective services programs provided by states and local governments. | $100 million for each of FY2011 through FY2014. |
| 6703(a) | New SSA Sec. 2042(c) | **Adult protective services demonstration grants.** Requires the Secretary to fund state demonstration programs for adult protective services that test methods to prevent and detect elder abuse. | $25 million for each of FY2011 through FY2014. |
| 6703(a) | New SSA Sec. 2043(a) | **Long-term care ombudsman program grants.** Requires the Secretary to award grants to improve the capacity of state LTC ombudsman programs to address abuse and neglect complaints, conduct pilot programs, and provide support for such programs. | $5 million for FY2011, $7.5 million for FY2012, and $10 million for each of FY2013 and FY2014. |
| 6703(a) | New SSA Sec. 2043(b) | **Ombudsman training programs.** Requires the Secretary to establish programs to provide and improve ombudsman training with respect to elder abuse, neglect, and exploitation for national organizations and state LTC ombudsman programs. | $10 million for each of FY2011 through FY2014. |
| 6703(b) | New authority | **National Training Institute for Surveyors.** Requires that the Secretary enter into a contract with an entity to establish and operate a National Training Institute for Federal and State Surveyors to provide and improve training of surveyors investigating allegations of abuse in programs and LTC facilities that receive payments under Medicare or Medicaid. | $12 million for the period of FY2011 through FY2014. |
| 6703(b) | New authority | **Grants to state survey agencies.** Requires the Secretary to award grants to state survey agencies that perform surveys of Medicare or Medicaid participating nursing facilities to design and implement complaint investigation systems. | $5 million for each of FY2011 through FY2014. |
| 6703(c) | New authority | **National nurse aide registry study and report.** Requires the Secretary, in consultation with appropriate government agencies and private sector organizations, to conduct a study on establishing a national nurse aide registry and report on its findings. | SSAN (no years specified) to carry out these activities, with funding not to exceed $500,000. |

**Source:** Table prepared by the Congressional Research Service based on the text of the Patient Protection and Affordable Care Act (ACA; P.L. 111-148, as amended).

## Table 10. ACA Discretionary Spending: Biomedical Research

| ACA Section | Statutory Authority (Agency) | Summary of Provision | Authorization of Appropriations; Funding (FY2011-FY2013) |
|---|---|---|---|
| 10409 | Amends PHSA Secs. 402(b) and 499(c); new PHSA Sec. 402C (NIH) | **Cures Acceleration Network (CAN).** Establishes a CAN program within the Office of the NIH Director to award grants, contracts, or cooperative agreements to support the development of treatments for diseases or conditions that are rare, and for which market incentives are inadequate. Eligible grantees include public or private entity, which may include a private or public research institution, an institution of higher education, a medical center, a biotechnology company, a pharmaceutical company, a disease advocacy organization, a patient advocacy organization, or an academic research institution. | $500 million for FY2010, and SSAN for subsequent fiscal years. Other funds appropriated under the PHSA may not be allocated to CAN. *FY2012 funding = $10 million, FY2013 request = $50 million.* |

**Source:** Table prepared by the Congressional Research Service based on the text of the Patient Protection and Affordable Care Act (ACA; P.L. 111-148, as amended).

## Table 11. ACA Discretionary Spending: Biologics

| ACA Section | Statutory Authority (Agency) | Summary of Provision | Authorization of Appropriations; Funding (FY2011-FY2013) |
|---|---|---|---|
| 7002 | Amends PHSA Sec. 351 (FDA) | **FDA approval of follow-on biologics.** Creates an abbreviated regulatory pathway for approving biological products that are demonstrated to be biosimilar to, or interchangeable with, an FDA-licensed biological product. Provides for the collection of user fees, subject to congressional authorization, to cover regulatory costs beginning in FY2013. [Note: On February 9, 2012, FDA released three guidance documents to assist industry in developing biosimilar products and submitting them to the agency for approval. See http://www.fda.gov/Drugs/DevelopmentApprovalProcess/HowDrugsareDevelopedandApproved/ApprovalApplications/TherapeuticBiologicApplications/Biosimilars/default.htm.] | SSAN for each of FY2010 through FY2012. |

**Source:** Table prepared by the Congressional Research Service based on the text of the Patient Protection and Affordable Care Act (ACA; P.L. 111-148, as amended).

## Table 12. ACA Discretionary Spending: 340B Drug Pricing

| ACA Section | Statutory Authority (Agency) | Summary of Provision | Authorization of Appropriations; Funding (FY2011-FY2013) |
|---|---|---|---|
| 7102 | Amends PHSA Sec. 340B(d) (HRSA) | **Improvements to 340B program integrity.** Requires the Secretary to develop systems to improve compliance and program integrity to (1) increase transparency and strengthen monitoring, oversight, and investigation of the prices that manufacturers charge covered entities; and (2) ensure covered entities do not divert drugs or obtain multiple discounts. Further requires the Secretary to establish a new administrative dispute resolution process to mediate and resolve covered entity overpayment claims and manufacturer claims against covered entities for drug diversion or multiple discounts. | SSAN for FY2010 and each succeeding fiscal year. *FY2011 funding = $4 million, FY2012 funding = $4 million, FY2013 request = $6 million (proposed new user fee program).* |

**Sources:** Table prepared by the Congressional Research Service based on the text of the Patient Protection and Affordable Care Act (ACA; P.L. 111-148, as amended). FY2011, FY2012 and requested FY2013 funding amounts are taken from HRSA's FY2013 congressional justification document, available at http://www.hrsa.gov/about/budget/index.html.

## Table 13. ACA Discretionary Spending: Medical Malpractice

| ACA Section | Statutory Authority (Agent) | Summary of Provision | Authorization of Appropriations; Funding (FY2011-FY2013) |
|---|---|---|---|
| 10607 | New PHSA Sec. 399V-4 (HRSA) | **Liability reform demonstration program.** Authorizes five-year demonstration grants to states for the implementation and evaluation of alternatives to current tort litigation for resolving disputes over injuries allegedly caused by health care providers or organizations. Planning grants of up to $500,000 may be awarded to states for the development of demonstration project applications. To receive a grant, a state must develop an alternative system that allows for the resolution of disputes caused by health care providers or organizations, and reduces medical errors by encouraging the collection and analysis of patient safety data related to the resolved disputes. | $50 million for the period FY2011 through FY2015. |

**Source:** Table prepared by the Congressional Research Service based on the text of the Patient Protection and Affordable Care Act (ACA; P.L. 111-148, as amended).

## Table 14. ACA Discretionary Spending: Pain Care Management

| ACA Section | Statutory Authority (Agency) | Summary of Provision | Authorization of Appropriations; Funding (FY2011-FY2013) |
|---|---|---|---|
| 4305(a) | New authority | **Conference on pain.** Requires the Secretary, within one year of appropriating funds, to contract with the IOM to convene a Conference on Pain for the purpose of assessing the public health impact of pain, reviewing pain research, care, and education, and identifying barriers to improved pain care. A report summarizing the Conference's findings must be submitted to Congress by June 30, 2011. [Note: IOM released its report on June 29, 2011. See http://painconsortium.nih.gov/.] | SSAN for each of FY2010 and FY2011. |

**Source:** Table prepared by the Congressional Research Service based on the text of the Patient Protection and Affordable Care Act (ACA; P.L. 111-148, as amended).

## Table 15. ACA Discretionary Spending: Medicaid

| ACA Section | Statutory Authority (Agency) | Summary of Provision | Authorization of Appropriations; Funding (FY2011-FY2013) |
|---|---|---|---|
| 2705 | New authority (CMS) | **Global payment system demonstration program.** Requires the Secretary, in coordination with the Center for Medicare and Medicaid Innovation, to fund up to five Medicaid demonstrations during the period FY2010 through FY2012 under which a participating state will adjust payments made to a large safety net hospital system or network from a fee-for-service model to a global capitated payment model. | SSAN (no years specified). |
| 2706 | New authority (CMS) | **Pediatric accountable care organization demonstration program.** Requires the Secretary to conduct a five-year Medicaid demonstration (Jan. 1, 2012 through Dec. 31, 2016) under which a participating state is allowed to recognize pediatric providers as an accountable care organization (ACO) for the purpose of receiving incentive payments. Eligible pediatric providers must meet certain performance guidelines established by the Secretary to be recognized as an ACO, and must achieve a specified minimum level of Medicaid savings to receive an incentive payment. | SSAN (no years specified). |

**Source:** Table prepared by the Congressional Research Service based on the text of the Patient Protection and Affordable Care Act (ACA; P.L. 111-148, as amended).

## Table 16. ACA Discretionary Spending: Medicare

| ACA Section | Statutory Authority (Agency) | Summary of Provision | Authorization of Appropriations; Funding (FY2011-FY2013) |
|---|---|---|---|
| 3129 | Amends and reauthorizes SSA Sec. 1820 (HRSA) | **Rural hospital flexibility grant program.** Extends authorization of appropriations for the rural hospital flexibility (Flex) grants that support a range of performance and quality improvement activities at small rural hospitals. Permits the funding to be used to help rural hospitals participate in delivery system reform programs authorized under ACA. | SSAN for each of FY2011 and FY2012, to remain available until expended.<br><br>*FY2011 funding = $41 million, FY2012 funding = $41 million, FY2013 request = $26 million.* [CFDA 93.241] |

**Sources:** Table prepared by the Congressional Research Service based on the text of the Patient Protection and Affordable Care Act (ACA; P.L. 111-148, as amended). FY2011, FY2012 and requested FY2013 funding amounts are taken from HRSA's FY2013 congressional justification document, available at http://www.hrsa.gov/about/budget/index.html.

## Table 17. ACA Discretionary Spending: Private Health Insurance

| ACA Section | Statutory Authority (Agency) | Summary of Provision | Authorization of Appropriations; Funding (FY2011-FY2013) |
|---|---|---|---|
| 1334 | New authority (OPM) | **Multi-state health plans.** Requires OPM to contract with health insurers to offer at least two multi-state health plans (at least one nonprofit) through exchanges in each state. Authorizes OPM to prohibit multi-state plans that do not meet standards for medical loss ratios, profit margins, and premiums. Requires multi-state plans to cover essential health benefits and meet all the requirements of a qualified health plan. | SSAN (no years specified). |

**Source:** Table prepared by the Congressional Research Service based on the text of the Patient Protection and Affordable Care Act (ACA; P.L. 111-148, as amended).

# Author Contact Information

C. Stephen Redhead, *Coordinator*
Specialist in Health Policy
credhead@crs.loc.gov, 7-2261

Kirsten J. Colello
Specialist in Health and Aging Policy
kcolello@crs.loc.gov, 7-7839

Elayne J. Heisler
Analyst in Health Services
eheisler@crs.loc.gov, 7-4453

Sarah A. Lister
Specialist in Public Health and Epidemiology
slister@crs.loc.gov, 7-7320

Amanda K. Sarata
Specialist in Health Policy
asarata@crs.loc.gov, 7-7641

# Acknowledgments

Pamela W. Smith provided extensive editorial comments during the development of the initial version of this report.

# Key Policy Staff

| Area of Expertise | Name | Phone | E-mail |
| --- | --- | --- | --- |
| Health Centers and Clinics | Elayne J. Heisler | 7-4453 | eheisler@crs.loc.gov |
| | C. Stephen Redhead | 7-2261 | credhead@crs.loc.gov |
| Health Care Workforce | Elayne J. Heisler | 7-4453 | eheisler@crs.loc.gov |
| | Bernice Reyes-Akinbileje | 7-2260 | breyes@crs.loc.gov |
| Long-Term Care | Kirsten J. Colello | 7-7839 | kcolello@crs.loc.gov |
| Prevention and Wellness | Sarah A. Lister | 7-7320 | slister@crs.loc.gov |
| Maternal and Child Health | Emilie Stoltzfus | 7-2324 | estoltzfus@crs.loc.gov |
| | Amalia Corby-Edwards | 7-0423 | acorbyedwards@crs.loc.gov |
| Health Care Quality | Amanda K. Sarata | 7-7641 | asarata@crs.loc.gov |
| Nursing Homes | Cliff Binder | 7-7965 | cbinder@crs.loc.gov |
| Health Disparities | Amalia Corby-Edwards | 7-0423 | acorbyedwards@crs.loc.gov |
| Emergency Care | Elayne J. Heisler | 7-4453 | eheisler@crs.loc.gov |
| Elder Justice | Kirsten J. Colello | 7-7839 | kcolello@crs.loc.gov |
| Biomedical Research | Pamela W. Smith | 7-7048 | psmith@crs.loc.gov |
| Biologics | Judith A. Johnson | 7-7077 | jajohnson@crs.loc.gov |
| 340B Drug Pricing | Cliff Binder | 7-7965 | cbinder@crs.loc.gov |
| Medical Malpractice | Vivian S. Chu | 7-4576 | vchu@crs.loc.gov |
| Pain Care Management | Kirsten J. Colello | 7-7839 | kcolello@crs.loc.gov |
| Medicaid | Cliff Binder | 7-7965 | cbinder@crs.loc.gov |
| Medicare | Sibyl Tilson | 7-7368 | stilson@crs.loc.gov |
| Private Health Insurance | Bernadette Fernandez | 7-0322 | bfernandez@crs.loc.gov |

www.ingramcontent.com/pod-product-compliance
Lightning Source LLC
Chambersburg PA
CBHW081405170526
45166CB00010B/3211